The Entrepreneur's Dilemma:

Short Stories To Guide Legal Decision-Making

Clarity ... From Start-Up To Succession

Effective legal help to obtain what you want and your business needs

Call our office today:

Griffin | A Professional Law Corp.

www.GriffinAPC.com

Make your appointment for a

FREE 30-MINUTE CONSULTATION

Our holistic approach will see you through from start to finish

DISCLAIMER PAGE

Additional copies are available at special quantity discounts for bulk purchases for sales promotions, premiums, fundraising, and educational use.

For more information, please contact:

GRIFFIN | A PROFESSIONAL LAW CORP.

Telephone: (866) 692-9913

Table of Contents

Introduction

We live in a country governed by laws. These rules act as a glue holding our society together, ensuring that, for the most part, people treat each other fairly, play by the rules, and hold up their ends of agreements.

Without laws – and contracts to enforce them – we would not enjoy the stability that we all take for granted. Commerce would be much more friction-filled. We'd have a harder time hiring people or building trust with new clients. When disputes would erupt, we'd fumble in the dark, reinvent the wheel and rely on corruption, arbitrary decisions, bias, and emotion to rule the day.

I love doing business with entrepreneurs because the work rhymes in many ways with what architects and engineers get to do.

Our work products, when done right, act like invisible shields. You don't want to think about a bridge's stability or a skyscraper's load-bearing capacity when you are driving over a bridge with your family or taking an elevator to the penthouse. You just expect success.

Likewise, the best contracts are the ones that effortlessly snap into place and never need to be "enforced." Why? Because they clarify exactly what parties to the agreement really want and need.

The Entrepreneur's Dilemma

Every great business relies on great contracts undergirding the operation. When I see a "mom and pop" shop better a market's goliath, obviously the owners deserve the lion's share of the credit. But some credit also goes to the "unsung heroes" who designed their agreements, so that business could get done smoothly according to their strategic plan.

Take the case of Karen, who started her own woodworking business. She processed so many orders through her personal website that she had to hire other people to fulfill customer requests. While Karen was an excellent technician, she didn't exactly relish dealing with paperwork. She got so caught up in the growth that she brought on two new workers, Nick and

Sheila, without having them sign any kind of working agreement.

On the third day of the job, Sheila cut her hand with a band saw and wound up in occupational therapy for three years.

Ultimately, the injury cost Sheila $20,000 in medical bills and related costs. Since Karen didn't have a contract with Sheila, the legal process to determine how to reimburse Sheila was long and painful.

Or consider Jonathan, whose personal consulting business was about to go up in flames, thanks to a war he got into with a vendor. The company suddenly tripled its prices and scrambled payment terms, just as Jonathan got hit with cash flow woes stemming from having hired two new people.

Jonathan wanted the vendor to comply with the terms established in the contract, but the vendor insisted on a work around.

Without careful negotiation, the blow up could lead to litigation and the downfall of both businesses – as well as downstream litigation from clients who didn't get their deliverables because of the dispute.

Ultimately, business contracts and transactional work are all about **people.**

- How should people behave towards one another in a business relationship and under what circumstances?

- What happens if there is a dispute?

- What terms should be set in place when two people (or two businesses) start working together?

- What can be done to maximize clarity – so that everyone involved in the deal knows exactly what's expected?

I feel privileged, because my team and I get to meet with people doing amazing things every day. We help these folks clarify, organize and prepare to do battle on behalf of important causes.

When a business owner is armed with the right contracts, they can negotiate from a place of strength, and that just feels great.

Normally, when I meet with business owners and their teams, I'd typically charge for that consultation, but as a thank you to you for investing time reading this book, I'd like to return the favor. Please flip to the end of the book to learn more about a unique offer to get insight into your most pressing contract project.

With that, let's dive in and talk about the most essential and interesting elements of business transactional work…

All About The Corporations, Partnerships And Other Business Structures You Can Form.

Kelly Anne was just getting started with her business. Her dad was an entrepreneur, and he often worked without protection from a corporate veil.

But Kelly Anne was more pragmatic; she knew she needed protection before she set up shop and took her idea to market. But the choices seemed endless... and complicated.

Should Kelly Anne operate as a sole proprietor or start a limited liability corporation (LLC), an S Corporation, a partnership, or some other structure?

The Entrepreneur's Dilemma

The answer, obviously, would depend on the nature of Kelly Anne's business, her personal assets and liability, her plans for growth, whether she had a partner or not and dozens of other factors.

One advantage of going the LLC route, for instance, as opposed to operating as a sole proprietor, is that the LLC owns the debts of the business. So let's say Kelly Anne rents out an office space in a downtown park through her LLC. And then she accidentally spills painting supplies and solvents on the ground when her truck hits a ridge. The property owner might sue to get payment for remediating the property. And let's say that price tag is a whopping $100,000. Who pays that bill?

If Kelly Anne is the sole proprietor, she would be on the line. But if her LLC rented the property, the company would own the debt. And if the company has only a few thousand dollars, that's all the owner could get. Kelly Anne wouldn't personally be on the hook for the $100,000 in clean up and remediation costs.

Obviously, no corporate protection is bulletproof. Depending on circumstances, Kelly Anne could still find herself on the business end of a lawsuit with her personal property on the line. Or a persistent creditor could find a clever way to pierce the corporate veil.

But being in business it's not about eliminating *all risk* – that's impossible. It's about identifying the most likely and most debilitating risks and mitigating against them in a smart, proactive, clear fashion.

Taking On Employees And Contractors To Grow Your Operation

Randall and Kendra were a husband and wife team that had taken over Randall's father's construction company and systematized it.

Now they wanted to expand. Thanks to some clever Internet advertisements, they had managed to secure a series of summer building contracts, but they didn't have enough of a labor force to get that work done efficiently — at least according to the timetable that their new customers had laid out. So they needed to hire help on short notice.

A business contract attorney could help Randall and Kendra design appropriate contracts for their short-term workers, so that the couple would stay in compliance with federal, state and local labor laws. The attorney could also make sure that the contracts used clear language, so that the workers understood their rights, responsibilities, and risks.

What's the point of this work? It's not just to protect against disaster (e.g. an employment or workers' comp lawsuit). It's also to tee up the relationships – to set expectations to make them more productive, pleasant and likely to succeed.

Aren't Oral Agreements Just As Good As Written Contracts In Some Cases?

Doing any business involves risk.

Especially at the beginning of a venture, when the strategy, tactics and model are all in flux, relationships will be at least somewhat ambiguous. Given this chaos, you might be tempted to opt for the proverbial "nod and a handshake" just to speed things up.

After all, in the start-up and rapid growth phases, friction can blunt momentum. If you over-structure a developing relationship, your ability to iterate and change your model gets blunted.

That said, the *lack* of using signed agreements can lead to big problems, both in the short and long term.

For instance, Carlos and his best friend from college, Ronnie, set up a software development company in their dorm room. They didn't think much about formalizing their partnership with one another. But as their company grew, and they built more products and got investors, Carlos and Ronnie started fighting over the direction of things.

Things came to a head when they got into an actual physical fight about whether to hire Ronnie's high school girlfriend as CMO. They decided to part ways. But because they hadn't established the terms of their partnership in clear, contractual language, the "business divorce" wound up incredibly messy, expensive and bitter.

There is another, subtler type of problem that will arise if you work habitually from handshake deals instead of contracts.

Case in point: Karen built her marketing empire on the backs of online freelancers that she curated and trained. In the beginning, Karen didn't have the resources or knowledge or foresight to use contracts. But after she got established, she looked around and saw that her business appeared to be "just fine" without having "all that paperwork hassle" in place.

So when she began to hire full time, in-house employees, she kept up this bad

habit of running her business without
using contracts with her employees.

Lo and behold, three months after
hiring her, Karen's secretary struck out,
claiming violations of the Fair Labor
Standards Act (FLSA), accusations that
Karen couldn't easily parry because
she had no written contract with the
secretary.

Do You *Really* Need An Attorney To Review Your Contracts Before You Sign Them?

Clarence inherited an agricultural machining business from his father, who in turn learned the ropes from his uncle more than half a century ago.

Fortunately for Clarence, the business systems remained intact from season to season, year to year. The company used a precise recipe to hire employees, bring in vendors, settle disputes, market its products at trade shows, etc.

So when Clarence made the decision to expand into a new niche in his Tri-State market, he didn't even think about reviewing his vendor contracts before piecing together the deal. Why bother? The machine worked.

But Clarence overlooked the fact that the neighboring state's (very different!) environmental and commerce laws would govern parts of the agreement.

Since Clarence was so comfortable with what had worked in the past – and what he had learned from his father and great uncle – he never thought to have an attorney vet the vendor contracts to determine the implications of such laws.

Minor point, right? Not so fast.

After the deal was inked, a third party vendor spilled agricultural byproducts onto a neighboring property. The pollution leached into the groundwater and affected several nearby farms.

The language of Clarence's old contract offered his company scant protection. Suddenly, he found himself embroiled in interstate environment litigation that ultimately cost his business over $400,000 in clean up fees and court costs.

All for want of a simple contract vetting.

Obviously, when you get into a completely *new* relationship or expand out your business model in a big way, you'll intuitively know to ask an attorney for contract help. You'll know to clarify terms and ideas – to make sure that you know exactly what you're agreeing to and what you're expecting of the other party.

But what Clarence's cautionary tale teaches us is that you must apply that same vigilance, even when a contract situation seems paint-by-numbers.

A microscopic amount of time spent with your attorney dotting every "i" and crossing every "t" is the key to confidence and peace of mind.

A parachutist must have complete confidence in her emergency chute to be able to jump out of the airplane completely focused and ready.

Likewise, you need to have complete confidence in your agreements, so you can focus like a laser on the real work.

If A Vendor Or Other Party Created A Contract, Do You Really Need An Attorney To Review It?

One of the mantras of modern entrepreneurship is *speed uber alles*.

You want to go fast, make mistakes, learn from those mistakes, recalibrate, create an action plan, and launch into motion.

You want to go through that cycle as rapidly as possible with as much learning as possible, so that you can eventually arrive at a model that has been forged by the crucible of the real world.

This "lean manufacturing" approach to running a business is intellectually seductive for many reasons.

   The Entrepreneur's Dilemma

However, the drive towards efficiency and speed can lead to vulnerability. For instance, to avoid even the hint of friction, you might just sign the contractual boilerplate that some vendor, supplier or freelancer serves up for you.

Elena runs an online art studio. She is always looking for distributors to help promote and sell her clients' works on other websites and galleries.

So when she met a prospective distributor at an art show who showed interest in her talent pool, she naturally got excited. She wanted to rush the business relationship and lock down that cash flow.

Fortunately, Elena had the good sense to avoid signing the distributor's contract before showing it to her friend, a contract attorney.

When Elena glanced at the language, it looked like standard boilerplate to her – i.e., legalese and gobbledygook. But her attorney friend pointed out that the contract was grossly unfair both to her and to her artist clients.

So Elena went back to the prospect and asked him to change certain language based on the advice of her attorney. She thought the negotiations wouldn't be a big deal. But the guy stalled. He refused to respond to Elena's notes and emails over the course of three weeks. Finally, when she sent a more firmly worded email

    The Entrepreneur's Dilemma

following up, he blew up! He lashed out at Elena and scuttled the deal.

Only *after* this outburst did Elena really do due diligence on the man. She discovered from other friends in her community that he had engaged in dubious business practices with people like her and cheated both artists and their reps.

By catching the red flags in the contract, Elena saved herself (and her artists) a great deal of panic, time and money.

WHAT HAPPENS WHEN A CONTRACT GETS BREACHED?

As we discussed earlier in the book, contracts exist to clarify business relationships and help them run smoothly.

But they also act in many ways like emergency safety nets – the kind acrobats use as they hop 30 feet above the floor on a string. They're there to catch you and save you when things slip.

When a party breaches your contract – fails to live up to terms or expectations – you can pull many possible remedies from your black bag. Let's take a look.

Sometimes it just takes a gentle reminder or a sensitive conversation to get the relationship back on track.

For instance, Angelica had a supplier that changed its billing terms without notifying her via email or phone. She suddenly saw charges on her credit card that she hadn't authorized. Angelica initially was really upset with this buyer, and she called the CEO to demand a refund. She even faxed him a copy of their contract with the billing arrangement highlighted and underlined for emphasis.

The CEO profusely apologized for the misunderstanding and agreed to respect the contracted arrangement in the future.
This honest mistake was easily course-corrected.

Sometimes, however, breaches can be much more challenging to fix.

Leonard and Lee ran a spice wholesaling business. They worked with a network of shippers and refiners in Europe and Central America to import spices, which they then packaged and marketed in the United States.

One day, Leonard and Lee got some unexpected bad news. One of their Portuguese connections, a major saffron supplier, had gone AWOL – completely off the radar. They received no explanation or advanced notice. Leonard and Lee had already paid for a large shipment of spice from this vendor, and they were on the hook to deliver product to several

     The Entrepreneur's Dilemma

regional hubs in the United States. They had a contract with the distributor, but *enforcing* that contract was another story.

The other party had literally abandoned shop, and so they had to wade into the choppy waters of international and Portuguese contract law.

Leonard and Lee would need to weigh the costs/benefits of pursuing a claim versus cutting their losses and moving on. A rough choice, but it illustrates an important idea.

In some cases, pursuing a breach of contract claim through aggressive means – negotiation, arbitration, or court action – can be more expensive than the remedy is worth to you.

Doing business carries irreducible risks, and even the most tautly constructed, clear and comprehensive contracts are not bulletproof vests. They can give you confidence to plow forward, but they can't protect you from everything.

How Frequently Do You Need To Update And Amend Your Contracts?

Far too many business owners have a "project" mentality when it comes to their contract agreements.

The underlying, unspoken belief is that contracts are things that can be "done once" and then forgotten about.

You recruit a new employee; he signs an agreement; and you're off to the races. You find a new vendor; you both hammer out an arrangement; and then you roll up your sleeves and get to work.

Sure, when *huge* transitions in the business occur, you will likely recognize that it's smart to review your contracts. For instance, you will reassess when you promote an assistant to an executive, recalibrate a deal with a key supplier or acquire a new company.

But the larger point is that contracts aren't static instruments! Like an estate plan or a marriage, an agreement acts like a stabilizing anchor. But the situation can change over time. It's not *"set it and forget it."* It's more like *"set it and forget it but review it occasionally as needed."*

Here's a story that demonstrates the dangers of standing still.
Diana's consultant shop helped brand local businesses to look more professional. To do this work, she cultivated relationships with lots of local printers, graphic artists, web people, etc. The contracts she used

                    The Entrepreneur's Dilemma

with these vendors were perfectly suited for her clients.

But as the consultancy expanded, Diana took on work with clients out of state. She never thought to rethink her contracts. Why fix what ain't broke?

But then a dispute with one of her artists led to an interstate court case over payment terms and who owned what pieces of some intellectual property. Diana's contract agreement was not enforceable because it didn't conform to the other state's legal requirements.

This led to a mess. Diana lost one of her best artists as well as a valuable client, all because her contracts were out of sync with where the business was.

WHAT ARE SIGNS THAT YOU NEED TO REVIEW YOUR CONTRACTS?

- You've identified a breach in a contract that has caused grief for you, a client or some other stakeholder.

- There's a substantial change in your relationship with an employee, vendor, supplier, partner or other stakeholder, such that the working relationship needs to be recalibrated.

- You've changed your business model or processes in a way that could affect contractual relationships. For instance, you start taking on out of state or international clients.

- You have developed or acquired a key piece of intellectual property that needs protection, such as a recipe for a special industrial solvent.

- State, local or federal laws have changed in ways that could affect your existing business relationships.

- Your company has gone through a major transition, such as a merger, acquisition, major downsizing, change of location, or radical change of business strategy.

- It's been a long time since you and your attorney have reviewed the contracts that your organization uses.

How Should You Find A Qualified Contracts Attorney?

Terrell knew it was about time to find an attorney.

He had made it through three grueling years of getting his company off the ground. He had hired a competent team to "mind the store," and he had worked feverishly to hammer his marketing and sales processes into place.

Terrell still fell nervous, though, that too many of his business relationships were poorly defined or defined ad-hoc.

He set about finding a contract attorney in a really intelligent way.

Before he gathered prospects via referrals or online searches, he first defined his key criteria.

He asked himself two big questions:

Why do I want a contract attorney?

I need someone to define the company's relationships, so that I can devote 100% of my time and energy to bringing in cash.

What characteristics do I need in my attorney?

Terrell developed a clever way to surface unspoken criteria he had in the back of his mind. He imagined what instructions he would give his sister, Julie, to do the recruiting for him.

- Find someone with extensive experience specifically in contract law, not just general business law.

- We want an attorney who is meticulous but who also will coach us about how to manage our agreements, and our business, going forward.

- We want someone who understands the plight of the entrepreneur, not just the business owner, and can truly be an advisor.

- While cost should be a consideration, we don't hire just on price alone. We need to get our legal strategy right.

- We want someone who has the ability to write in clear, plain language (as opposed to legalese) and who can also explain complex contract terms to us in language we (and our partners, clients, vendors, etc.) can understand.

Only *after* Terrell defined his purpose and standards did he cast his net looking for prospective contract lawyers.

And then he cast a *wide* net. He looked to friends and entrepreneurs for references, searched online for inspiration, and got insights from his business coach.

Next, using the criteria he had developed upfront, he narrowed the pool of prospective attorneys down to three, and then he set up consultations with each law firm.

Prior to these meetings, Terrell wrote down an extensive list of questions as well as a statement of his needs and concerns. That way, he could communicate exactly what he needed and expected.

At the consultations, he took careful notes about the *substance* of the lawyers' answers as well as subtle details, such as whether he got a good vibe or not.

After that leg work, he went over his notes, consulted with his business coach, and chose an attorney who "got" him and his business on a deep level.

    The Entrepreneur's Dilemma

After retaining the lawyer, he listened carefully to what the attorney needed from him and followed up on his designated tasks.

As a result, Terrell revised, amended and added contracts as needed and created a powerful stabilizing framework that let his business grow and take strategic risks.

What Does Our Law Firm Provide?

At Griffin, A Professional Law Corp., we've created a unique approach to supporting our client's business goals.

Our firm has developed partnerships to help maximize the way we can support your business through success.

First, we are primarily engaged in transactional work. This means that we don't take many cases to Court for litigation.

We prefer to strategize a way to avoid the expense of litigation where at all possible.

Second, our attorneys also hold a real estate license. This ensures that we are extremely familiar with terms in most of the typical contracts used for

The Entrepreneur's Dilemma

purchasing or leasing real estate and can assist you in your own purchase/lease negotiations as business or family needs grow or shift.

Third, we have an association with Aftokrat Academy LLC that provides our clients with the benefit of gaining preferred pricing on membership to their business growth platform. So that, as your business grows, we'll be there to help you plan for the future business you continue to create!

Take Action

As we end, I want to thank you again for taking the time to read this brief guide to business dilemma's faced by entrepreneurs.

Whether you need to create a whole catalogue of agreements for a growing business, triage after a breach of contract or go to court to deal with a serious dispute, I would like to help.

Normally, I charge for consultations with prospective clients. But I would like to offer you, as a thank you, a chance to get this initial consultation at no cost to you. Just mention that you read this book when you call the office at (866) 692-9913, and we will waive your fee.

   The Entrepreneur's Dilemma

Call now, and let's talk. This private, confidential consultation will give you the peace of mind and confidence you need to face down whatever you're up against. You do not have to go through this alone. Get the help you need and deserve now!

Matthew Murillo
Family Business Attorney

Take action today toward

YOUR NEW FUTURE!

Call our office TODAY!

Make your appointment for a

FREE CONSULTATION

Find RELIEF

And Get Back In Control of Your Future!

Call: (866) 692-9913

GRIFFIN | A PROFESSIONAL LAW CORP.

www.GriffinAPC.com

I will share all of your options.

Your Future Awaits!